Canada in the 21st Century

Ontario

Suzanne LeVert

George Sheppard
Upper Canada College
General Editor

CHELSEA HOUSE PUBLISHERS
Philadelphia

Opposite: Ice fishing is a popular pastime on the many small lakes in Ontario.

Chelsea House Publishers
EDITOR IN CHIEF: Stephen Reginald
MANAGING EDITOR: James D. Gallagher
PRODUCTION MANAGER: Pamela Loos
ART DIRECTOR: Sara Davis
DIRECTOR OF PHOTOGRAPHY: Judy Hasday
SENIOR PRODUCTION EDITOR: J. Christopher Higgins
ASSISTANT EDITOR: Anne Hill
PRODUCTION SERVICES: Pre-Press Company, Inc.
COVER DESIGNER/ILLUSTRATOR: Forman Group

First Printing
1 3 5 7 9 8 6 4 2

The Chelsea House World Wide Web address is http://www.chelseahouse.com

Library of Congress Cataloging-in-Publication Data
LeVert, Suzanne.
    Ontario / Suzanne LeVert ; George Sheppard, general editor.
        p. cm.—(Canada in the 21st century)
    Includes bibliographical references and index.
    ISBN 0-7910-6068-3
        1. Ontario—Juvenile literature. [1. Ontario. 2. Canada.] I. Sheppard,
George. II. Title. III Series.

F1057.4 .L49 2000
971.3—dc21

00-040523

Contents

My Canada

by Pierre Berton

"Nobody knows my country," a great Canadian journalist, Bruce Hutchison, wrote almost half a century ago. It is still true. Most Americans, I think, see Canada as a pleasant vacationland and not much more. And yet we are the United States's greatest single commercial customer, and the United States is our largest customer.

Lacking a major movie industry, we have made no widescreen epics to chronicle our triumphs and our tragedies. But then there has been little blood in our colonial past—no revolutions, no civil war, not even a wild west. Yet our history is crammed with remarkable men and women. I am thinking of Joshua Slocum, the first man to sail alone around the world, and Robert Henderson, the prospector who helped start the Klondike gold rush. I am thinking of some of our famous artists and writers—comedian Dan Aykroyd, novelists Margaret Atwood and Robertson Davies, such popular performers as Michael J. Fox, Anne Murray, Gordon Lightfoot, k.d. lang, Céline Dion, and Shania Twain, and hockey greats from Maurice Richard to Gordie Howe to Wayne Gretzky.

The real shape of Canada explains why our greatest epic has been the building of the Pacific Railway to unite the nation from

sea to sea in 1885. On the map, the country looks square. But because the overwhelming majority of Canadians live within 100 miles (160 kilometers) of the U.S. border, in practical terms the nation is long and skinny. We are in fact an archipelago of population islands separated by implacable barriers—the angry ocean, three mountain walls, and the Canadian Shield, that vast desert of billion-year-old rock that sprawls over half the country, rich in mineral treasures, impossible for agriculture.

Canada's geography makes the country difficult to govern and explains our obsession with transportation and communication. The government has to be as involved in railways, airlines, and broadcasting networks as it is with social services such as universal medical care. Rugged individualism is not a Canadian quality. Given the environment, people long ago learned to work together for security.

It is ironic that the very bulwarks that separate us—the chiseled peaks of the Selkirk Mountains, the gnarled scarps north of Lake Superior, the ice-choked waters of the Northumberland Strait —should also be among our greatest attractions for tourists and artists. But if that is the paradox of Canada, it is also the glory.

Cypress Lake is just one example of Ontario's beautiful landscapes. Without doubt, mountains, lakes, and forests are among the province's most valuable assets.

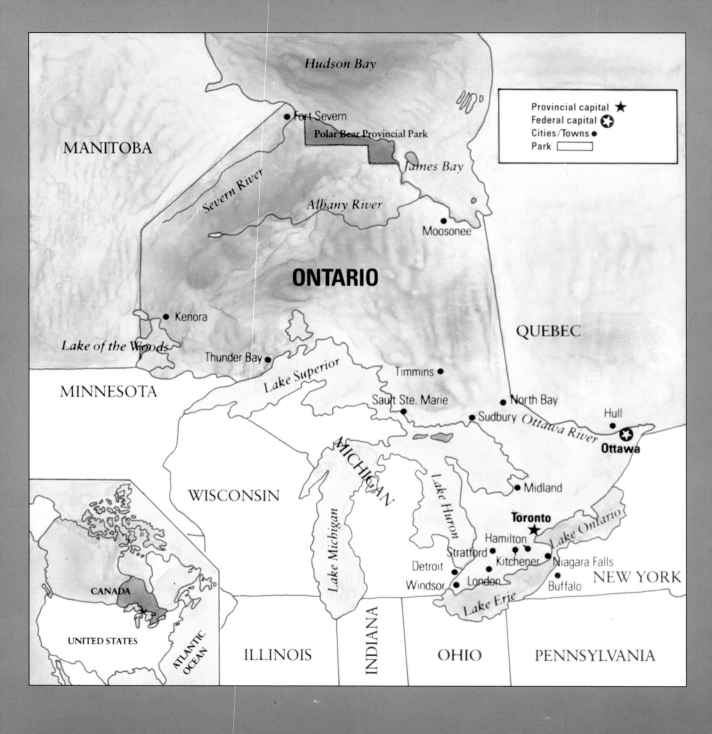

Eastern White Pine

White Trillium

Ontario at a Glance

Population: 11,513,800
Area: 412,582 square miles (1,068,582 km)
Capital: Toronto
Flower: white trillium (white lily), adopted 1937
Gem: amethyst
Tree: eastern white pine
Bird: common loon (under consideration)
Flag: adopted May 21, 1965
Provincial Motto: Ut inceptit fideles sic permanent (Loyal she began, loyal she remains)
Major crop: tobacco

Government: parliamentary system; lieutenant governor, nominal head of government, appointed by federal government; premier, head of ruling party, holds real power with self-chosen executive council from among members of his/her party in the one-house Legislative Assembly or provincial Parliament. A 104-member Assembly is elected by popular vote by district. Ontario citizens also elect 103 members to the federal House of Commons.
Major industries: automobiles, paper products

The Land

Rich in resources and vast in size, Ontario is known as Canada's heartland. Seat of the nation's capital, Ottawa, and home to more than one-third of the nation's population, Ontario's landscape also includes Canada's fastest growing, most cosmopolitan city, Toronto, as well as its most fertile farmlands and richest mineral deposits. Ontario's magnificent waterways and its proximity to the United States have made this province the economic and cultural center of the country.

Almost 1,300 miles (2,100 km) from east to west and 1,000 miles (1,600 km) from north to south, Ontario is the second largest province in Canada. With a total area of 412,582 square miles (1,068,582 sq. km), Ontario is twice as big as the state of Texas, three times as big as the country of Japan, and is larger than Germany, France, and Italy combined.

Ontario is practically an island. Its southern border consists of 2,360 miles (3,800 km) of freshwater coastline formed by the St. Lawrence River and four of the Great Lakes: Ontario, Erie, Huron, and Superior. Its northern border is formed by the James and Hudson Bays, a 680-mile (1,094-km) saltwater coast.

Algonquin Park, *left, is* one of 130 provincial parks that show off Ontario's natural beauty. Nearly 70 percent of Canada's vegetables are grown on farms in southern Ontario, *above.*

To the west lies Ontario's neighboring province, Manitoba, and to the east, the Ottawa River and the province of Quebec.

Ontario might also be called a land of contrasts, for with its great area come different climates and landscapes. Divided into two distinct regions, northern and southern, Ontario has polar bears and gold mines to the north and rattlesnakes, peach orchards, and tobacco farms to the south.

One reason for this great environmental diversity can be traced back to prehistoric times. More than 10,000 years ago, Ontario was buried under a glacier 3 miles (4.8 km) deep that covered most of North America during the last Ice Age. This glacier completely reshaped the land it covered, and its departure exposed the Pre-Cambrian, or Canadian, Shield, a mass of rock formations at least 600 million years old.

The Canadian Shield, one of northern Ontario's most important geological features, is a huge, horseshoe-shaped basin that covers almost half of Canada. Though the Shield is sometimes called Ontario's treasure chest because of its rich deposits of iron, nickel, and other precious metals, the soil in this area is poor in nutrients and full of rocks, making farming difficult.

In the south, however, the retreat of the glaciers left behind nutrient-rich soil. Warmer than the north and with an abundance of fertile farmland, southern Ontario is the agricultural center of the province, with cattle ranches, fruit orchards, vineyards, and vegetable farms. In fact, southern Ontario is called the Banana Belt because of its mild climate.

The Waterways

Ontario is an Iroquois Indian word meaning "Shining Lake" or "Beautiful Waters," a most appropriate name considering that more than 19 percent of the province's surface area is water. Dotted with more than 250,000 lakes and with some of the continent's mightiest rivers, the province of Ontario has a history shaped in large part by these waterways.

Historically, rivers and lakes provided Ontario's first highways, bringing settlers from Europe and the United States into its vast interior. Even today, waterways are a main source of transportation. Major ports on the Great Lakes handle cargo by the millions of tons. Oceangoing vessels can travel from the Atlantic Ocean to the head of Lake Superior using the St. Lawrence River and its artificial extension the St. Lawrence Seaway. The Ottawa River, one of the longest in Canada, is the boundary between the provinces of Ontario and Quebec. To the north, the Albany River leads from the province's center to the Atlantic Ocean through James Bay.

With the magnificent Parliament Buildings towering above, the Rideau Canal serves as one of Ottawa's most delightful recreation areas, with pleasure boats cruising in the summer and skaters gliding in the winter. Completed in 1831, the Rideau Canal was created to allow British ships to avoid American gunboats poised on the St. Lawrence River.

With water comprising more than 19 percent of Ontario's surface area, sailboats like this one on Georgian Bay are familiar sights.

The huge bodies of water surrounding Ontario moderate the province's climate. Although the winters can be quite frigid in the far north, where the temperatures average between 12 degrees and –9 degrees Fahrenheit (–11 degrees to –23 degrees Celsius), the rest of the province has more moderate winters, with temperatures averaging 25°F (–4°C).

Perhaps Ontario's most outstanding geological feature is another legacy from the Ice Age: the Niagara Escarpment, a plateau that extends for about 250 miles (400 km). Its centerpiece is Niagara Falls, one of the world's greatest waterfalls, located on the border between New York State and Ontario. Some 15 million cubic feet (425,000 cubic meters) of water per minute—500,000 tons—tumble over two precipices on either side of the international border.

Located on the Niagara River, an important trade route, the Falls are bypassed by ships through a remarkable canal. When a freighter goes around Niagara Falls, it climbs "stairs" called locks to get from Lake Ontario to Lake Erie. A ship is lifted from one level to the next by canal operators raising the water level in the locks.

Ontario's natural resources—its mineral deposits in the Canadian Shield, its fertile soil to the south, and its magnificent waterways—combine to make this province a rich and fruitful "heartland" indeed.

The thundering waters of Niagara Falls, one of the great natural wonders of the world, attract thousands of tourists every year. Niagara Falls is also an important hydroelectric energy source for Ontario and surrounding areas.

The History

Some 10,000 years before the first Europeans arrived in Canada, three distinct groups of native Americans settled in Ontario. Not much is known about these earliest inhabitants except that they, like all native Americans, probably migrated from Asia after the last Ice Age. In the east and to the north lived Algonquian-speaking people (Chippewa, Cree, Ojibwa, and Mississauga) who called themselves "Anishinabe." In the southwest of what would become Ontario lived Iroquoian-speaking native Americans. The largest of this group, who called themselves "Wendat," were known as Hurons by the Europeans. Finally, the "Inuit" lived in the far north; they were called Eskimos by their neighbors. By the time the Europeans arrived in the 16th century, the Indian population in the land now known as Ontario numbered approximately 50,000 to 60,000.

Samuel de Champlain, *left,* was probably the first European to see the land that would become Ontario when he sailed up the St. Lawrence River in 1608.

Pioneer Days

"Canada is useful only to provide me with furs" is a quotation attributed to Madame de Pompadour, the mistress of French King

Louis XV. Indeed, European greed for fur and other natural wealth, such as lumber and fish, motivated the explorers and early pioneers to stake their claims in this region of the New World.

French explorer Samuel de Champlain was probably the first European to see the land that would become Ontario. In 1608, he sailed up the St. Lawrence River and started a settlement in what is now Quebec. A dynamic and inspired young lieutenant of Champlain's, 17-year-old Étienne Brulé, is credited with being the first white man to explore the region west of Quebec. He was the first to see the heartland of Ontario: the forests and farmland around Lake Ontario, Lake Erie, and the north shore of Lake Superior.

Ontario's many rivers acted as highways for pioneers and native populations alike, allowing them to settle deep in the wilderness.

At the same time, the British began their own settlements. Henry Hudson arrived in Ontario in about 1609 by way of the great body of water to the north that now bears his name, Hudson Bay. Hudson died there, in fact, after his crew mutinied. He and seven others were set adrift in a small boat and left to die.

Slowly, despite attacks from the French, the British established trading posts along the shores of Hudson Bay. One of these trading companies, now known as Hudson's Bay, became one of the most powerful in the world. Britain's disregard for any French claims to the prosperous fur trade aroused extreme hostility among the French, who had, after all, reached Ontario first. The battle between them for control over this rich new land is an integral part of Ontario's history. For many decades, the territory between Hudson Bay in the north and the French forts in the south was fiercely disputed.

Relations between the European traders and the native population were at first quite friendly. Without help from the Indians in the ways of the wilderness, it is doubtful that the early visitors could have survived. Trading between the two groups prospered as well, with the French and British exchanging knives, cloth, and other goods for the Indians' valuable beaver pelts.

But wars among the tribes over trading rights with the newcomers took their toll on the native population. The rivalry between the people of the Iroquois Confederacy, who lived south of Lake Ontario, and their relatives, the Huron, had a great effect on Ontario's history. While the French established a close bond with the Huron, the Iroquois formed relationships with Dutch and British traders who were eager to get in on the fur trade.

Battles between the two Indian groups raged for years, until the Iroquois scored a decisive victory at a French mission called Sainte-Marie Among the Hurons. Headed by a courageous priest, Father Jean de Brébeuf, the mission had been established by French Jesuits in 1639. In 1648 and 1649, the Iroquois devastated the fort and captured, tortured, and killed Father Brébeuf before finally forcing 350 survivors to leave the settlement altogether.

Perhaps even more crucial to the course of Indian history in Ontario and elsewhere, Europeans brought with them many diseases that were lethal to the Indians, who had no immunity to them. No one knows just how many thousands of Huron, Iroquois, Cree, and other tribe members were wiped out by smallpox and measles.

Resentment of the white man's intrusion into their land and their cultures caused many native Americans to turn against the settlers. Like his fellow Frenchman, Father Brébeuf, Étienne Brulé met his death at the hands of native Americans after spending years living among various tribes.

After the Huron were dispersed, the absence of any dominant tribe in southern Ontario made this land especially attractive to settlers. Eventually, greed for more and more territory would cause the Euroamericans to push the remaining Indian population onto separate parcels of land, called reserves.

Loyal she began, loyal she remains

The struggle for New France, as Canada was then known, became part of the Seven Years' War between France and Britain (1756–63). The North American phase of the war was called the French and Indian War and many of its battles were fought in what is now Ontario.

In 1759, the French were roundly defeated by British General James Wolfe in a decisive battle at Quebec. Wolfe's victory made New France part of the British Empire. Within two decades, however, some American colonists decided to seek independence from Britain. The American Revolution not only brought the United States into being but also led to the formation of a new English-speaking colony north of the Great Lakes. After the British were defeated, thousands of pro-British refugees, known as Loyalists, flooded into the region—10,000 in 1783 alone—bringing not only their families and their hunger for land but also their staunch loyalty to Britain. *Ut inceptit fideles sic permanent* (Loyal she began, loyal she remains) is still the provincial motto.

The leader of the Six Nations Indians in New York State, Joseph Brant, was granted land in Ontario by the British after fighting on their behalf during the American Revolution. He led some 1,600 Iroquois Indians to settle in the province during the late 1700s.

Along with a grant of land, each new Loyalist arrival was given an axe, a spade, and other tools necessary for starting a new life in the wilderness. There was now little threat from the few Indians who lived in the region. In fact, many of the Loyalists were themselves native Americans who had fought on the side of the British during the Revolution. Under the leadership of Joseph Brant, an Iroquois chief, some 1,600 members of the Iroquois Confederacy also moved north to take up residence in British territory.

Shortly after their arrival, the Loyalists made it clear that the French civil law that still governed Quebec was not suitable for them. With the Constitutional Act of 1791, a separate province, Upper Canada (now Ontario), was formed from the territory west of the Ottawa River. The land east of the river would be known as Lower Canada (today's Quebec).

Although it may seem extraordinary today, the first Canadians were quite fearful of an invasion by the United States. Upper Canada's first capital was at Niagara-on-the-Lake, just across the border from New York. But John Graves Simcoe, Upper Canada's first lieutenant governor, felt that such a location was too close to the United States for comfort. In 1797, he officially moved the capital to York, at the site of Old Fort Toronto, some 90 miles (140 km) to the north across Lake Ontario.

In the meantime, the fur trade was still flourishing in the northwest. Originally divided fairly evenly between the French and the English, the fur trade was challenged by a group of aggressive Scotsmen who gave the established traders a run for their money. The Scots formed the North West Company, thereby increasing the number of settlements in the north. The Nor'Westers, as they were nicknamed, established Fort William on Thunder Bay in 1801. Bitter fights between British and Scottish traders ensued until, in 1821, the Hudson's Bay and North West companies merged.

The War of 1812

In June 1813, a settler named Laura Secord walked nearly 20 miles (32 km) through enemy lines to warn British troops that the

John Graves Simcoe was appointed Ontario s first lieutenant governor after the Constitutional Act of 1791 divided New France into two provinces, Upper Canada (now Ontario) and Lower Canada (now Quebec).

Winters were long and bitterly cold for Ontario's first settlers.

enemy—United States soldiers—had arrived in the area. Though Indian spies may already have warned the British commander of the attack, Laura Secord become a heroine of the War of 1812.

When war was declared between Britain and the United States in 1812, the dispute was apparently over shipping rights. The United States, however, saw the war as a chance to drive the British out of Upper Canada once and for all. Lieutenant Governor Simcoe's worst fears were realized when the United States invaded.

Many Upper Canadians, however, did not want to go to war. In fact, Upper Canada was, at this time, more "American" than British. The population of approximately 70,000 was almost completely made of settlers from the United States. Most feared a conflict with their increasingly powerful neighbor to the south. The British army in Upper Canada, however, was better trained than U.S. forces, and over the next two years they were able to prevent a takeover of the province.

Although these skirmishes did not claim many casualties or change the international boundary, they did reinforce loyalty to the British Crown among the Ontario population. Immigration from the United States was strictly limited after the war, but settlers from Great Britain arrived by the thousands. In addition, many Scottish and English soldiers as well as German mercenaries who fought in the war decided to stay. Later, after the famine in Ireland during the 1840s, Irish from both the Protestant north and the Catholic south immigrated to Canada. Once here, the Protestant Irish helped to further strengthen the pro-British spirit in the province.

The city of Ottawa, on the eastern shore of the Ottawa River, was made the Dominion's national capital in 1867.

Confederation and Reform

Because so many of the colonists had witnessed the birth of a democracy in the United States, a push for democratic reforms began soon after in Upper Canada. Although Upper Canada had a legislative assembly elected by the people, real political power lay in the hands of the lieutenant governor. Upper Canada's supreme leader, hand-picked by the British Crown, the lieutenant governor ruled along with his executive council, which he selected himself. Many believed that this arrangement, known as the Family Compact because of its exclusivity, was corrupt and inefficient.

Reformers from all over the province petitioned the British Crown. In 1837, a rebellion by several hundred Upper Canadians was quickly crushed, but not without initiating some reforms. In 1841, Upper Canada and Lower Canada were joined and renamed Canada West (later Ontario) and Canada East (later Quebec). By the 1850s, however, great strides had been made in reorganizing Upper Canada's system of government. Elected politicians, not appointed officials, decided most issues of importance.

In the meantime, other colonies throughout the huge expanse that is Canada had been gaining in population and power. For many reasons, a yearning to confederate—to unite—was growing among the colonies. One reason was a fear of an increasingly powerful United States, which the Canadians felt might again invade. The prospect of greater economic power also led to calls for confederation.

The Dominion of Canada

In 1867, the British Parliament, for these same economic and security reasons, agreed to unite the provinces of Nova Scotia, New Brunswick, Canada West, and Canada East into the Dominion of Canada. Canada West, now with a population of more than one and a half million took back its original name, Ontario, "Shining Lake."

The system of government set up in the new Dominion of Canada was based largely on the parliamentary system of Great

Britain. Each province would have its own government elected by the general population. In addition, the people would elect representatives to the national government. The city of Ottawa on the eastern shore of the Ottawa River, which had been named by Queen Victoria to be the capital of the united provinces of Canada West and East in 1867, became the Dominion's national capital. Toronto remained Ontario's provincial capital.

Set atop the highest point in the city, the Parliament buildings, the seat of the national government, form one of Ottawa's most dramatic architectural landmarks.

Today, Ontario's government is multilayered. The center of this structure is the provincial government, which exercises great power. This power stems from the economic control the government has over the province's land and natural resources. The use of all minerals, forests, and wildlife is controlled and administered by the provincial government.

Though the lieutenant governor, now appointed by the federal government, is still technically the head of Ontario's government, real power lies with the premier (known as the prime minister until the title was changed in 1972). He or she works closely with a provincial cabinet, which the premier chooses from among members of his or her party in the popularly elected 104-member legislative assembly. The provincial government is responsible for the administration of health and education, property and civil rights, and the judiciary. It also has the power to collect taxes from provincial citizens.

Old Fort William, located in Thunder Bay, was the center of the fur trade in Ontario's northwest. A fully costumed staff and an authentically detailed reconstruction recall the exciting pioneer days of the early 1800s.

In addition, the province is divided into counties and municipalities, each of which has its own council to attend to the needs of its communities. Cities and towns are governed by a mayor and municipal council. This level of government concerns itself with police, transportation, and other local matters. This strong and stable system of government has been a key to Ontario's development.

To preserve its long and rich history, Ontario has reconstructed many of its old forts and villages. A daily changing of the guard at the Fort Erie restoration brings back the days when British soldiers staved off American troops during the American Revolution and the War of 1812.

The Economy

One of the first chores of the new Confederation, and one that propelled Ontario into its position as Canada's economic heartland, was the building of a railway to span the entire breadth of the nation. The Canadian Pacific Railway (which spanned the country by 1885) opened up Ontario's manufacturing, resource, and trade potential.

Today Ontario is served by two east-west interprovincial railroads. The province also has one north-south line, the Ontario Northland Railway. Up north, the ONR is also known as the Polar Bear Express because it ends at the pioneer town of Moosonee, one of the northernmost points in the province. Trains on this line, which stop at mileposts to pick up prospectors or drop off hunters, fishermen, and sightseers, helped to open up the mining and the paper industries.

In fact, the history of Ontario during the 20th century has a great deal to do with its growth as the industrial center of the nation. After the railways, it was the introduction of hydro-electricity—energy generated by Ontario's most plentiful resource, water. In 1906, businessmen prevailed on the provincial

Spanning 1,300 miles (2,100 km) from east to west and 1,000 miles (1,600 km) from north to south, Ontario depended upon the construction of an extensive railway system to enhance its development. *At left,* a train speeds through the Agawa Canyon. Fresh peaches, grapes, strawberries and other fruits thrive in southern Ontario, especially around Niagara-on-the-Lake, *above.*

The nickel and copper capital of Canada, Sudbury is a thriving industrial city located in Ontario's northeast. Paper and construction materials are also manufactured in this city of 92,059 people.

government to step in to help finance and organize a hydroelectric resource, just as the federal government had done to help build the railroads. As a result, the Hydro-Electric Power Commission (now Ontario Hydro) was established and was soon providing a surplus of cheap energy. Ontario Hydro spurred the growth of manufacturing, mining, and refining.

The timber and paper industries also flourished with the help of the provincial government. In 1898, the government first took control of timberland not already privately owned. Before then, timber could be cut and exported—mainly to the United States—at will. Although attempts have been made

to conserve and replenish Ontario's forests, extensive logging has seriously depleted this most valuable resource.

Gold, silver, and other precious metals enhance Ontario's standing as Canada's heartland. Deep deposits of copper, zinc, and other base minerals are also important to the province's industrial growth. Although mineral deposits were first discovered in the mid- to late 1800s, it was in the period following World War II that Ontario's real mineral boom occurred. One of the most important finds was the largest uranium deposit in the Western world, discovered at Elliot Lake in 1953.

Ontario's agricultural base is broader and more profitable than that of any other Canadian province. Nearly 70 percent of Canada's vegetables and almost all of its tobacco, soybeans, and corn are grown in Ontario. More than 100 crops and commodities are produced, mainly in the south's fertile soil. Grapes, strawberries, and other fruits thrive around Niagara, the region that produces some of the country's finest wines. Approximately two-thirds of Ontario's agricultural wealth comes from livestock and dairy products. Poultry and egg production is also an important aspect of the province's farm income.

In addition to harvesting the province's mineral, timber, and other natural resources, Ontario in the 20th century became Canada's industrial center. Automobile manufacturing is the province's most important industry, producing more than 90 percent of all transportation equipment made in Canada. Huge steel mills in southern Ontario process iron ore mined in Nova Scotia and other parts of Canada, as well as from other countries. Today, nearly 60 percent of Canada's steel requirements are met in Ontario.

Just as in the United States, however, it is the service industries— finance, education, health care, advertising, real estate, restaurant and hotel services, publishing and other media—that account for most of the province's economy. More than 67 percent of Ontario's gross domestic product (the total value of goods and services produced within the province in a year) comes from service-related employment.

Despite its great economic wealth, Ontario faces some serious problems common to most modern industrialized societies, such as overcrowded cities and pollution. But its manufacturing base remains strong, producing 52 percent of Canada's manufactured goods and 80 percent of its manufactured exports. Ontario looks to the new century with excitement, yet will continue to be challenged by the problems of success.

Toronto, the provincial capital, is Canada's largest, most populated city. At its center are the twin towers of Toronto's City Hall, completed in 1965.

The People

Once, at the very beginning of Ontario's history, the British, French, and native Americans made up its entire population. Today, Ontario is one of Canada's most ethnically diverse provinces. Just since the end of World War II, immigration and other trends have more than doubled its population. People from all over the world have flocked to Ontario by the hundreds of thousands.

Ontario remains home to nearly 160,000 native American Indians, more than any other province. Most Indians live in the northwest on reserved lands that cover approximately one and a half million acres (710,000 hectares).

Life for the native people remains bleak. For more than 200 years they have been politically, economically, and culturally isolated. It was not until 1960, for instance, that native Americans living on reserves were allowed to vote in provincial elections. Native Americans, in Ontario and elsewhere, have among the highest infant mortality rates and lowest life expectancy rates in the world.

In recent decades, however, a healthy resurgence of native culture and political participation has occurred. Ancient arts and

Native American arts and crafts, such as the leather work pictured *at left,* are still widely practiced. The annual "sugaring off" of maple syrup, *above,* is one of Ontario's enduring traditions.

Toronto's answer to Mardi Gras is Caribana, a festival celebrating the city's rich West Indian culture, represented here by a parade participant in colorful costume.

crafts have been revived, and negotiations between tribes and the provincial government over land rights are now taking place.

Public Life

In addition to its economic opportunities, Ontario has many other things to offer its citizens. Chief among these is education, Ontario's number one budgetary expense.

Free education for all is provided through Ontario's more than 4,000 public schools and 1,500 Catholic schools. For higher education, Ontario has 17 degree-granting universities and 24 community colleges; all are publicly funded.

An extensive public health care system is another of the province's highlights. The government-administered Ontario Health Insurance Plan provides free health care to all citizens. More than 250 public hospitals, funded by the government, are operated throughout the province—from the thousand-bed University Health Network hospitals to tiny clinics in remote villages.

High technology has hit Ontario with full force, adding an important element to the province's economy. Computer courses have become more prominent at the universities and community colleges.

Communities

Most Ontarians, some 90 percent, live in just 10 percent of the province's territory. The area around Toronto, especially to the southwest along the shoreline of Lake Ontario, is the most densely populated in all of Canada.

Life for urban Ontarians is similar to that of most North American city dwellers. They work in manufacturing or service industries, commute on subways or buses or in private cars, and live in apartments, condominiums, and private homes. But even

Winter sports take the chill off Ontario's long winters. Skiing is popular throughout the province.

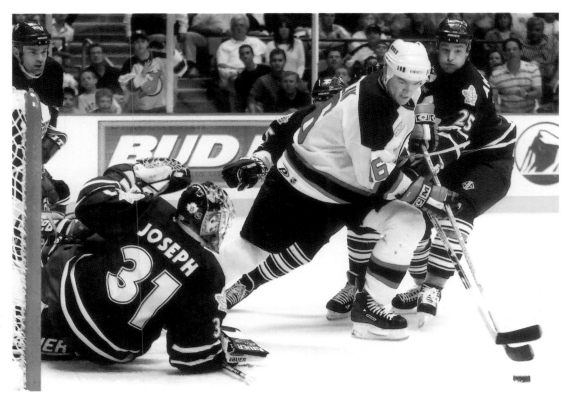

New Jersey Devils center Bobby Holik (C) gets a point blank shot off on Toronto Maple Leafs goalie Curtis Joseph (L) as Leafs defenseman Greg Andrusak (R) tries to battle for the puck during the first period of Game 6 of their NHL Eastern Conference playoff series at Meadowlands Arena May 8, 2000. Joseph made the save on the play.

though they live in densely populated areas, urban dwellers in Toronto and Ottawa are never more than an hour's drive from vineyards, cattle ranches, and other agricultural settings.

For those million or so Ontarians who make their homes in the rugged north, everyday life is not very different from that of their southern neighbors. Though their air is cleaner and their streets less crowded, many northern cities such as Sault Ste. Marie, Thunder Bay, and Sudbury have a cosmopolitan air to them. Mainly miners, lumberjacks, and mill workers, northern Ontarians are accustomed to long winters and hard work. Their reward is to live amid some of the most beautiful forests and lakes in the world.

The bounty from southern Ontario's rich soil finds its way to grocery stores and farmers' markets, such as this one at Hamilton, throughout the country.

Leisure Time

Sports are at the top of most every Ontarian's list of favorite things to do. Whether watching or participating, Ontarians are among the world's most avid sports fans. The Toronto Blue Jays play major league baseball and the Ottawa Senators and Toronto Maple Leafs are the province's gift to Canada's national passion for ice hockey. The Toronto Rock of the National Lacrosse League have won two championships and football is also big business in Ontario. It is home to the Toronto Argonaut and Hamilton Tiger-cat teams in the Canadian Football League's Eastern Division.

Ontarians also take advantage of the hundreds of parks and other recreational facilities abounding in the countryside. In addition to four national parks within its borders, Ontario operates some 130 provincial parks. The largest, the Algonquin Park, covers nearly 3,000 square miles. The province's 250,000 lakes and many rivers and streams provide vacationers with fishing, swimming, and boating in the summer and icefishing and snowmobiling in the winter.

The Arts

Actors, writers, filmmakers, and painters have all found inspiration and support in Ontario. In its cities as well as in the countryside, Ontario—especially in its capital, Toronto—is a center for the arts in Canada.

In painting, it was the Group of Seven, working in the early 1900s, who first defined a specifically Canadian style. Using the lush wilderness of Algonquin Park, these mostly landscape painters, including Lawren Harris and Tom Thomson, took bold approaches to color and imagery. During the 1950s, a new style based on abstract expressionism emerged from a group of Toronto artists, the Painters Eleven.

The world's most comprehensive collection of Canadian art is found in Ottawa's National Gallery of Canada, which also has extensive European and Asian collections.

In literature, modern fiction writers of international renown include Alice Munro, Margaret Atwood, and the late Robertson Davies. Marshall McLuhan was a philosopher concerned with modern communications, and Donald Creighton was a historian and biographer; both of these writers were born and worked in Ontario.

Perhaps the most famous theatrical event in Ontario is the Shakespeare Festival, which stages about six Shakespearean plays a year. Located in the quaint little town of Stratford, this festival attracts thousands of theatergoers a year. In addition, theater companies by the dozen bring plays and musicals to audiences in Toronto, Ottawa, and Ontario's smaller cities. During the many festivals held throughout the province, more remote villages and towns enjoy Ontario's touring companies.

Displaying cultural artifacts, internationally acclaimed works of art, dinosaur bones, and the latest high-tech inventions, museums in Ontario, like the National Gallery of Canada in Ottawa and the Royal Ontario Museum in Toronto, are world-class. Reconstructed pioneer settlements and native American villages help bring the past to life and keep Ontario's unique heritage a vital part of its future.

Music and dance also thrive in Ontario. Ontario has more than 30 symphony orchestras, including the Toronto Symphony, the Hamilton Philharmonic, and the National Arts Center Symphony, based in Ottawa. Toronto's National Ballet of Canada, formed in 1950, is recognized as one of the world's premier companies.

Music, dance, and theater flourish in Ottawa, Toronto, and in smaller communities throughout Ontario. The Shakespeare Festival, *at left,* is an annual event of international renown that takes place in the town of Stratford.

The Cities

Whether in cities of 10,000 or less or in the huge metropolis that is Toronto, almost 90 percent of Ontarians today live in urban centers. These cultural and financial centers have grown from small trading posts during pioneer days into modern, ethnically diverse, exciting communities.

Toronto

Modern Canada's largest and most cosmopolitan city had rather humble, not very promising roots. Known as "Muddy York" when John Graves Simcoe first chose it as the provincial capital in 1797, Toronto was ugly and, it was said, boring. During a visit to the city in the early 1900s, poet Rupert Brooke wrote, "The only depressing thing is that it will always be what it is, only larger."

Toronto proved its critics wrong. Today, it is recognized as a first class city, as dynamic as any in the world. In the past few decades, it has become the heart of the nation's cultural, financial, and industrial institutions. It is Canada's principal wholesale and

Once a small, ugly city known as "Muddy York," Toronto, *at left,* is now one of the world's great cities, an exciting center for the arts and industry. One of Ottawa's notable attractions is its National Aviation Museum, *above.*

retail center and one of its busiest ports. The Toronto Stock Exchange is the largest in Canada and one of the most important in North America. High technology international companies, such as Honeywell, IBM Canada, and Canada Systems Group make Toronto their headquarters in Canada.

Four and a half million people now live in "Muddy York" and its suburbs, which started out in 1867 with just 50,000 settlers. What is most interesting, perhaps, is that two-thirds of this population comes from somewhere else. There are more Italians living in Toronto than anywhere, outside of Italy, more Portuguese than anywhere else in North America, and more Chinese than anywhere else in Canada.

Despite its vast population, Toronto is, by all accounts, a pleasant place to live. Its architecture is stunning, marked by modern glass and steel skyscrapers speckled with historic buildings dating back to the 1700s. Its subway system, called the TTC (Toronto Transit Company), is clean and safe and is used by millions of people every year. And although crime is an issue in every large city, Toronto is relatively safe; it has just a fraction of the crime rates of the neighboring U.S. cities of Buffalo and Detroit.

Frequently called Hollywood North, Toronto's film industry is exceptionally active. *Three Men and a Baby* and *Dead Ringers* were two recent American hits shot in and around Toronto. Television filming is also big business: "Night Heat" and "Degrassi Junior High" were two American favorites filmed in Ontario's capital.

Toronto's museums are also first rate. The Royal Ontario Museum, the largest in Canada and the second largest in North America (only New York's Metropolitan Museum is bigger), has more than 6 million items in its various collections. The Art Gallery of Ontario, nearly a century old, now has more than 24,000 paintings, sculptures, and prints by such esteemed artists as Rembrandt, Renoir, and Picasso. The AGO, as it is known, also has one of the most extensive collections of Canadian art and artifacts in the country.

Ottawa's many parks, such as this one on Parliament Hill, *opposite,* allow city dwellers to enjoy the outdoors within city limits.

Ottawa

A native American word meaning "a place of buying or selling," Ot-tawa did not have a very promising start. When Ottawa became the capital of the Dominion of Canada, it was a small backwoods town with little to recommend it save its prime location on the Ottawa River. A thriving city of more than 300,000 people today, Ottawa's population numbered just 7,500 when it was first incorporated.

The Parliament buildings, huge stone structures set atop a bluff overlooking the Ottawa River, form Ottawa's most dramatic landmark. It is in these Gothic buildings that the national government is administered. Representatives from all over Canada meet in these buildings to make federal laws, decide how to spend federal money, and oversee the administration of justice—quite a challenge considering the diverse needs and politics of this huge nation's 10 provinces and three territories.

Despite the concentration of federal power here, Ottawa is very much a part of the province of Ontario. It sends elected officials to the provincial capital of Toronto and contributes taxes to the provincial treasury. Yet there is a distinctly different feeling to this city, due in large part to its unique location.

Situated on the border between Ontario and Quebec, Ottawa is a bridge between the two founding cultures of Canada, French and English. Although it is primarily an English-speaking city, Ottawa is also home to a very large French-speaking population served by three French television stations, a French newspaper, bilingual street signs, and extensive French education programs. The University of Ottawa is fully bilingual.

Thanks to extensive urban planning, Ottawa remains one of the most graceful cities in North America. Rejecting glass and steel canyons in favor of elegant avenues and lush, green parks, Ottawa has retained an appealing Old World flavor. The Rideau Canal connects the Rideau and Ottawa rivers and is one of the city's foremost landmarks. Opened in 1832, the canal was built so that ships could avoid traveling on the St. Lawrence River, where they might be attacked by the United States. Today its stone bridges and enchanting lights add to Ottawa's beauty.

Other Cities of the South

London: Located on the Thames River in one of North America's most fertile regions, London has a population of more than 250,000. It is a vibrant, growing city with both contemporary and traditional architecture and activities and is home to the University of Western Ontario. Its industries include iron, textiles, and food processing. It is also known as the Forest City because of its abundance of beautiful trees.

Hamilton: At the center of the "Golden Horseshoe"—the half-moon-shaped strip of industry and wealth that stretches from Oshawa east of Toronto to St. Catharines to the west—Hamilton is the steel capital of Canada. With more than 300,000 people, Hamilton is a study in contrasts. Gritty and tough with steel mills dominating the skyline, Hamilton also is home to the spectacular Royal Botanical Gardens, 2,000 acres (810 hectares) of colorful flower displays and a wildlife sanctuary. McMaster University, a host of museums, and a symphony orchestra combine to make Hamilton one of Ontario's most diverse cities.

Windsor: Canada's most important automobile manufacturing city is located within a few miles of the United States's automotive capital, Detroit, Michigan. The area that is now Detroit-Windsor was first explored by the French as early as 1640. The French established settlements there in 1701, but Windsor itself was not incorporated until the 1830s. When Henry Ford crossed the Great Lakes to open a Canadian branch of the Ford Motor Company there in 1928, the once modest village began to grow into one of Ontario's major cities.

The French influence is still quite strong in this city of about 200,000 people, and Windsor has been designated a bilingual-bicultural area by the federal government. Windsor also has a strong bi-national tradition as well: Every year it co-hosts with

First established as a fur-trading post by the French in 1678, Thunder Bay is now northern Ontario's most populous city and a vital industrial center. The largest grain-handling port in the world, Thunder Bay has a population of more than 100,000.

Detroit the International Freedom Festival to celebrate both countries' "birthdays."

Thunder Bay

Northern Ontario's most populous city, Thunder Bay lies at the western terminus of the St. Lawrence Seaway, some 900 miles (1,500 km) from Toronto and Ottawa. It is a fairly new city, incorporated in 1970 when the communities of Port Arthur and Port William were joined. But the history of this city of more than 100,000 people is a long one, one that tells much of Ontario's northwestern story.

Established by the French in 1678 as a fur-trading post, this early settlement was one of the first to be acquired by the aggressive Scottish North West Trading Company. The Scots named it Fort William, after the governor of the powerful company, William McGillivray. In 1884 silver was discovered at a nearby settlement, which was then named Port Arthur, in honor of Queen Victoria's son, Prince Arthur. Thunder Bay was not named until 1970.

Drastic changes occurred in the intervening years. In addition to its status as Canada's third largest port, this bustling city claims to be the largest grain-handling port in the world. Its re-creations of Old Fort William and its excellent ski resorts make it a tourist haven for thousands of visitors every year.

Other Cities of the North

Sudbury: During its early years, timber was Sudbury's main industry, but ever since copper ore was discovered in the mid-1880s, Sudbury has been known as the nickel and copper capital of Canada. The Sudbury Basin provides approximately one-quarter of the Western world's output of nickel and 4.2 percent of its copper, about 30 percent of Canada's total copper production. But Sudbury, with a population of about 90,000 people, is more than a mining town. It boasts both a university and college, is home to the tourist destination Science North, and is the center of Ontario's northeastern trading region. Other industries include the manufacture of paper, building supplies, and construction materials and the production of sulfuric acid.

Sault Ste. Marie: The site of a French mission in the 1600s, "The Soo" is the site of one of the most active canals in the entire St. Lawrence Seaway system. Linking Lakes Huron and Superior, the locks at Sault Ste. Marie are vital to Canada's shipping. More than 80,000 people make their home in this quaint city, which is also a major center of steel manufacturing at the Algoma plant. Sault Ste. Marie, Ontario, is joined by a bridge with its twin city, Sault Ste. Marie, Michigan.

Things to Do and See

- **Algonquin Provincial Park,** northeast of Toronto: 3,000 square miles (7,600 km) of wilderness with eight compounds, three lodges, and canoe routes and hiking trails galore.
- **African Lion Safari and Game Farm,** near Hamilton: 750 exotic animals and birds roam freely on large reserves.
- **Bell Homestead,** Brantford: The home of Alexander Graham Bell is now a telephone museum.
- **Canadian War Museum,** Ottawa: The history of Canada's fighting men and women—complete with weapons from Indian clubs to guided missiles.
- **Ontario Science Centre,** Toronto: More than 800 hands-on exhibits of the wonders of science and technology.
- **Casa Loma,** Toronto: This fairy-tale castle was built by multimillionaire Sir Henry Pellatt, who spent $3 million to furnish his medieval creation with gold-plated bathroom fixtures and one of the first private elevators in the world.

Museums for every interest and taste can be found in Ontario. One young lady, *opposite,* had a hair-raising adventure when she took part in a static electricity experiment at Toronto's Science Center.

Weaving and other crafts are practiced and displayed in Ontario's many pioneer villages, such as Upper Canada Village near Toronto.

- **Old Forts and Pioneer Villages:** Fort Erie, Fort George near Niagara-on-the-Lake, Fort William in Thunder Bay, and Fort York in Toronto are just a sampling of the province's preserved or reconstructed forts. Sainte-Marie Among the Hurons near Midland and the Black Creek Pioneer Village in Toronto are just two of many reconstructed villages.

- **Ontario Place,** Toronto: A waterfront amusement park on Lake Ontario, offering man-made beaches, the world's largest movie screen, and an outdoor amphitheater called the Forum that seats 8,000 people.

- **Royal Ontario Museum,** Toronto: Canada's largest museum, with extensive natural history collections and a world-famous Chinese art gallery. Adjacent is the Children's Museum.

- **International Hockey Hall of Fame,** Kingston: The birthplace of Canada's national sport is celebrated at this museum, which follows the game's development through equipment, photographs, and artifacts.
- **National Aviation Museum,** Ottawa: Canada's past and future in aviation is exhibited with full-size replicas, video and audio presentations, and prints.
- **Amethyst Mines,** Thunder Bay: Visitors pick their own official provincial gemstone when they visit these open-pit mines and displays.
- **Horseshoe Falls:** 2,600 feet (792 meters) wide and 173 feet (53 meters) high, Niagara Falls is the centerpiece of southern Ontario.

Formed about 10,000 years ago, the falls at Niagara now generate well over 3 million kilowatts of power and provide an intriguing international border between Canada and the United States.

Festivals & Holidays

Winter, spring, summer, and fall, Ontarians celebrate their ethnic diversity, natural beauty, and cultural heritage.

Winter: Ontario's winter wonderland is revealed in a number of different festivals. Christmas is celebrated on December 25; December 26 is Boxing Day. Niagara Falls holds a **Winter Festival** in mid-January. **The Bon Soo Winter Carnival** in Sault Ste. Marie at the end of January features a torchlight parade followed by polar bear swims, sled dog races, and parades.

Spring: Elmira hosts a "sugaring off" at the **Maple Festival** in April. Niagara has a **Blossom Festival** to celebrate the coming of spring, followed by the blooming of 3 million tulips at the **Ottawa/Outaouais Festival of Spring.** Queen Victoria's birthday is celebrated with fireworks and parades throughout the province.

Summer: In June, the Stratford Shakespeare Festival begins its season on the banks of the Avon River. July 1, **Dominion Day** or **Canada Day,** is marked by parades and fireworks. At the **International Freedom Festival,** Windsor, Ontario, and Detroit, Michigan, join together to celebrate their countries' birthdays. July finds Toronto in full Caribbean regalia during **Caribana,** a Mardi Gras-like festival of West Indian culture. At the beginning of August, the **International Sailing Regatta** at Lake of the Woods in far western Ontario draws huge crowds. Brantford hosts the **Six Nations Pageant,** a celebration of Iroquois culture and arts. The **Canadian National Exhibition,** one of the world's largest agricultural, technical fairs, takes place from mid-August to Labor Day.

Fall: The **Algoma Arts Festival** brings theater, music, and art shows to Sault Ste. Marie in mid-September. The **Canada Grand Prix** car race is held at Mosport. **Oktoberfests** in Kitchener and London bring Canada's German heritage alive every October. Oshawa has a magnificent **Fall Flower Show** early in November.

Ontario's dynamic German heritage comes alive during Kitchener's Oktoberfest, an annual opportunity to celebrate with festivals and parades.

Fun Facts and Famous People

- Alexander Graham Bell, a Scotsman, invented the telephone at Brantford, Ontario, in 1874.
- North America's first commercial oil wells were developed in Petrolia, Ontario, in 1857.
- The Dionne quintuplets were born in Callander, Ontario, in 1934.
- Billed as the longest street in the world, Yonge Street runs approximately 1,000 miles (1,600 km) from the north shore of Georgian Bay to downtown Toronto.
- Lacrosse is the oldest sport in Ontario. It was played by the Huron and Iroquois before Europeans arrived.
- Among Ontario's many medical discoveries are the heart pacemaker (developed at the University of Toronto), cobalt treatments for cancer patients, and insulin for the treatment of diabetes.
- Hockey player Wayne Gretzky, singer Shania Twain, news anchorman Peter Jennings, comedians Dan Aykroyd, John Candy, Alan Thicke, and Martin Short, actors Lorne Greene, Raymond Massey, and Christopher Plummer, and impressionist Rich Little have all been famous in the United States—and they were all born in Ontario.
- Emma Goldman, famed American feminist and anarchist, died in Toronto in May 1940.
- Hockey's most coveted trophy, the Stanley Cup, is displayed at the Hockey Hall of Fame in Toronto.
- The world's second-largest McDonald's fast-food restaurant is located in Toronto, on the grounds of the Metro Zoo.
- The Rideau Canal in Ottawa is billed as the longest skating rink in the world.

Although born in Scotland and an American citizen, Alexander Graham Bell spent many years living in Ontario. He invented the telephone and other new technologies while living in Brantford, *above*.

Opposite: In winter, Ottawa's Rideau Canal freezes over, forming the world's longest skating rink.

Chronology

1608	Samuel de Champlain sails up the St. Lawrence River.
1609	Henry Hudson sails into Hudson Bay. His men mutiny and he and seven others die.
1668	The first Hudson's Bay Company fur-trading station is built on James Bay.
1783	Loyalists from the United States settle in Ontario following the American Revolution.
1791	Upper Canada (Ontario) separates from Lower Canada (Quebec).
1812	U.S. forces invade Ontario during the War of 1812.
1827	The first college in the province, the University of Toronto, is established.
1842	Queen's University is founded in Kingston.
1857	Queen Victoria names Ottawa the capital of Canada.
1867	Ontario joins the Canadian Confederation as one of the first four provinces.
1883	Nickel ore is discovered at Sudbury.
1928	Ontario's automobile industry begins in Windsor.
1945	Canada's first nuclear reactor starts operations near Chalk River.
1959	St. Lawrence Seaway opens.
1979	North York, a former borough of Toronto, becomes Ontario's newest city.
1989	The Skydome, the world's only multipurpose stadium with a retractable roof, becomes home to the Toronto Blue Jays.
1992	The Toronto Blue Jays win the World Series of Major League Baseball and repeat as champions in 1993.
1998	An ice storm brought 100 millimeters of freezing rain to eastern Ontario. Tens of thousands of houses were left without power and heat. Damage topped $1 billion.

Further Reading

Glazebrook,, G. P. de T. *Life in Ontario: A Social History*. Toronto: University of Toronto Press, 1968.

Hagan, John; Mosher, Clayton James. *Discrimination and Denial: Systemic Racism in Ontario's Legal and Criminal Justice Systems, 1892–1961*. Toronto: University of Toronto Press, 1998.

Hocking, Anthony. *Ontario*. Toronto: McGraw-Hill Ryerson, 1979.

Law, Kevin. *Canada*. New York: Chelsea House, 1990.

McNaught, Kenneth. *The Penguin History of Canada*. New York: Penguin, 1988.

Malcolm, Andrew. *The Canadians*. New York: Random House, 1985.

Marleau, Jason. *Backroad Mapbook: Ontario Cottage Country*. British Columbia-New Westminster: Mussio Ventures Ltd., 1998.

McConnell, Barbara; Michael Odinse. *Sainte-Marie Among the Hurons*. Toronto: Oxford University Press, 1980.

Morrison, Samuel Eliot. *Samuel de Champlain: Father of New France*. Toronto: Little Brown, 1972.

Scadding, Henry. *Toronto of Old*. Toronto: Oxford University Press, 1966.

Seibel, George A. *Ontario's Niagara Parks, 100 Years: A History*. Ontario, Canada: Niagara Parks Commission, 1985.

Shepherd, Jennifer. *Enchantment of the World: Canada*. Chicago: Childrens Press, 1987.

Sheppard, George. *Plunder, Profit and Paroles: A Social History of the War of 1812 in Upper Canada*. Montreal-Kingston: McGill-Queen's Press, 1994.

Woodcock, George. *The Hudson's Bay Company*. New York: Macmillan, 1970.

Woodcock, George. *The Canadians*. Cambridge: Harvard University Press, 1979.

Index

ACKNOWLEDGMENTS
All photos courtesy of Industry, Science and Technology Canada except: illustrations on page 7 by Debora Smith; drawings on pages 14 and 59 courtesy of the Bettmann Archive; photo on page 58 courtesy of National Capital Commission; drawings on pages 16, 19, 21, 22, 23 courtesy of the National Archives of Canada; photo on page 37 courtesy of Popperfoto/Archive Photos; and photo on page 39 courtesy of Reuters/Archive Photo.

Suzanne LeVert has contributed several volumes to Chelsea House's CANADA IN THE 21ST CENTURY series. She is the author of four previous books for young readers. One of these, *The Sakharov File,* a biography of noted Russian physicist Andrei Sakharov, was selected as a Notable Book by the National Council for the Social Studies. Her other books include *AIDS: In Search of a Killer, The Doubleday Book of Famous Americans,* and *New York.* Ms. LeVert also has extensive experience as an editor, first in children's books at Simon & Schuster, then as associate editor at *Trialogue,* the magazine of the Trilateral Commission, and as senior editor at Save the Children, the international relief and development organization. She lives in Cambridge, Massachusetts.

George Sheppard, General Editor, is an instructor at Upper Canada College in Toronto. Dr. Sheppard earned his Ph.D. in Canadian History at McMaster University in Hamilton, Ontario and has taught at McMaster, Laurentian, and Nipissing Universities. His research specialty is Canadian Social History and he has published items in *Histoire sociale/Social History, The Canadian Historical Review, The Beaver, Canadian Social Studies, The Annual Bulletin of Historical Literature, Canadian Military History, The Historical Dictionary of the British Empire, The Encyclopedia of POW's and the Internment,* and *The Dictionary of Canadian Biography.* He has also worked as a historical consultant for educational material in both multimedia and print format and has published a book entitled *Plunder, Profit and Paroles: A Social History of the War of 1812 in Upper Canada.* Dr. Sheppard is a native of Timmins, Ontario.

Pierre Berton, Senior Consulting Editor, is the author of 34 books, including *The Mysterious North, Klondike, Great Canadians, The Last Spike, The Great Railway Illustrated, Hollywood's Canada, My Country: The Remarkable Past, The Wild Frontier, The Invasion of Canada, Why We Act Like Canadians, The Klondike Quest,* and *The Arctic Grail.* He has won three Governor General's Awards for creative nonfiction, two National Newspaper Awards, and two ACTRA "Nellies" for broadcasting. He is a Companion of the Order of Canada, a member of the Canadian News Hall of Fame, and holds 12 honorary degrees. Raised in the Yukon, Mr. Berton began his newspaper career in Vancouver. He then became managing editor of *McLean's,* Canada's largest magazine, and subsequently worked for the Canadian Broadcasting Network and the *Toronto Star.* He lives in Kleinburg, Ontario.